The Gluten-Free Lunch Book

The best lunch and snack ideas
to stay gluten-free

One-in-ten people react to gluten.
One-in-one hundred have coeliac disease.

Are you the one?

If so, then you will want to go gluten free.
This book tells you how to solve the lunch problem!

Enjoy staying gluten-free!

www.doctorgluten.com

The Gluten-Free Lunch Book

The best lunch and snack ideas
to stay gluten-free
Authors: Chris Ford & Dr Rodney Ford
Copyright 2006 RRS Global Ltd.

National Library of New Zealand Cataloguing-in-Publication Data

Ford, Chris, 1954-
The gluten-free lunch book : best lunch and snack ideas to stay
gluten-free / Chris Ford & Rodney Ford.
ISBN 0-473-10498-9
1. Gluten-free diet—Recipes. 2. Gluten-free foods.
3. Lunchbox cookery. I. Ford, Rodney, 1949- II. Title.
641.56318—dc 22

Published by RRS Global Ltd.
PO Box 25-360, Christchurch, New Zealand
www.doctorgluten.com

Printed by Tien Wah Press.
Singapore

Jacket cover, art work and illustrations
by Liz Fazakarley of *Ford Design*.

Contents

Lunch ideas with children in mind

What can you have for lunch?

This book is written especially for parents who have gluten-free children. It is also for anyone who wants to continue to stay gluten-free.

From our long experience of looking after people who are on gluten-free diets, the "lunch problem" is always the sticking point. "What can I eat for lunch?!" is the common cry.

Thinking up what you make for lunch becomes tricky. What do you give children for lunch so that you are not repeating the same thing day after day? What can you take for your lunch at work that is easy? What morsel does not require an oven or microwave to heat it up? Lunches at home are easier than having a packed lunch.

This book will solve your lunch problem. It will help you to have a well balanced and fun lunch each day. We give you a wide variety of lunch ideas for lunch boxes, school lunches, work lunches, picnics and snack times. Now you know what you can have for lunch when you are following a strict gluten-free diet.

We hope you will enjoy these lunch suggestions. They are gathered under appropriate headings which you will find easy to follow.

We thank the many parents and colleagues who have helped us gather together all of these ideas into one book. Enjoy!

The gluten problem – staying gluten-free

Why are you gluten-free?

Before you commit to being strictly gluten-free, you should first reconsider your reasons for your life without gluten. If you are sure of your reasons, then you will be strongly committed to keep gluten-free.

We have found that about one person in every ten should be on a gluten-free diet. Some research groups say that gluten-sensitivity is even more common.

One in ten people react to gluten

There are many reasons to go on a gluten free diet:

1. The most common medical indication is for coeliac disease (also called gluten-sensitive enteropathy). This is when the gluten in your food damages your small bowel. This condition is usually completely cured by a strict gluten-free diet. About one in every one hundred people is affected by coeliac disease. However, many such people are without symptoms. If you have this condition, then you need to be a on a strict gluten-free diet, lifelong. The diagnosis requires blood tests and an endoscopy (small bowel biopsy).

2. Having gluten-sensitivity is the most common reason for people to go gluten-free. Gluten-sensitivity occurs when gluten causes a host of symptoms and illness which can be completely reversed when you go gluten-free. This is best diagnosed with a blood test (the IgG-gliadin antibody test).

3. It is a good idea to delay the introduction of gluten into the diets of babies and young children who have a strong family history of coeliac disease or gluten-sensitivity. In a family that is gluten-free, it is not difficult to keep young children gluten-free for the first few years of their lives. We advise keeping such children off gluten until they get to three or four years old.

4. Some people opt for a gluten-free diet simply for a healthy lifestyle choice. A gluten-free diet is a very healthy diet. Gluten is not necessary part of your diet. There are excellent and nutritious food replacements for all of the gluten products. Most people on a gluten-free diet are more aware of the value of eating well and they usually make expert food choices.

What is gluten?
What is this substance that you are so strenuously trying to avoid? Gluten is a complex mixture of proteins that is found in the grains of wheat, barley and rye. Therefore, *any* food that is made from these cereals will contain gluten. For instance, it is found in wheat flours, bread, pasta, cookies, biscuits, cakes, muffins, pancakes, and pastry – and so on. But you can easily do without it.

Unfortunately, gluten is also put into foods as a "food additive". Gluten is very useful. It gives added flavour and a pleasing texture to your food. It is added to countless processed foods. You need to be suspicous of all processed foods as they might contain a gluten additive. It therefore takes quite a lot of trouble to completely avoid gluten in your diet.

Details about finding hidden gluten, useful lists of gluten-free foods and help on setting up your pantry are in our book:
"Going Gluten-Free: How to get started".

Are you gluten-sensitive?

You are gluten-sensitive if you get symptoms from eating gluten. The great difficulty that we all have is to recognise if we are *normal*.

Most people just put up with their chronic symptoms in the belief that their troubles are to be endured. It is part of our culture. Most people do not recognise that they have symptoms that can be cured. Most of these symptoms are due to gluten! Western diets contain lots of wheat, which contains lots of gluten. Therefore, most people eat gluten at most meals. Also, gluten-laden foods are increasing in our diets due to the growth of the fast-food and convenience-food markets.

Yes! Most people think that they are *normal*. They just put up with tiredness, lethargy, mood problems, headaches, gastric reflux and sore tummies. They are unaware that gluten might be undermining their health. They have never been gluten-free. Therefore, they cannot tell how great they would feel if they cut gluten out of their diet.

What are gluten-sensitive symptoms?

Symptoms from gluten are so wide-ranging that they are so often overlooked. These symptoms are listed on the next page. The number one symptom is tiredness, lethargy and lack of energy. Gut problems often dominate. Brain disturbances are very common.

Recognise your symptoms

One-in-ten people are gluten-sensitive. It is very common. It could be affecting you! So, check out your symptoms on the list. If you can tick *any* box, then you could be gluten-sensitive.

Gluten-sensitive symptoms

Do you or your family have any of these problems?

☐ tired, exhausted, lethargic
☐ uncomfortable tummy
☐ bloating and gas troubles
☐ gastric reflux or heartburn
☐ diarrhoea or constipation

☐ unhappy with your weight
☐ not growing well
☐ eating problems
☐ lack of energy
☐ weakness

☐ runny nose and sinus problems
☐ chronic iron deficiency
☐ osteoporosis, bone and joint pains
☐ dermatitis, eczema or bad skin
☐ infertility

☐ headaches or migraine
☐ feel depressed or moody
☐ find it hard to think clearly
☐ poor sleep

☐ hyperactive or cranky
☐ Attention Deficit Hyperactivity Disorder (ADHD)
☐ autism
☐ mental health problems

If you can answer "yes" to one or more of these problems, then you (or your child) have a high chance of being gluten-sensitive.

The ten gluten-sensitive target organs

There are a many organs in your body that can be badly affected by gluten. In the diagram, the ten target organs are indicated by the diamond boxes. The small bowel (coeliac disease) is only one of these ten target organs. These ten organs are:

Gut related symptoms
1. Mouth   – ulcers, runny nose, sore throat.
2. Oesophagus   – gastro oesophageal reflux, heart burn, swallowing difficulties.
3. Stomach   – indigestion, slow emptying, gastritis.
4. Small bowel   – coeliac disease (enteropathy), malabsorption, diarrhoea.
5. Colon   – diarrhoea and constipation, bloating, low immune function.
6. Rectum   – constipation, soiling (encopresis).

Other symptoms
7. Brain   – disturbed behaviour, migraine, headache, depression, mood disorders, ataxia, autism, epilepsy, Attention Deficit Hyperactivity Disorder (ADHD).
8. Skin   – Dermatitis Herpetiformis, eczema.
9. Immune   – run-down, low immunity, recurrent infections.
10. Growth   – poor height and weight (short and/or thin).

Nutritional consequences

In addition to damage to these target organs, there are the nutritional consequences of a poorly functioning gut. These problems include:

Bones and joints   – osteoporosis, bone and joint pain.
Nutritional deficiency – anaemia, osteoporosis, low levels of vitamins and minerals.
Immune deficiency   – run-down, recurrent infections.
Infertility

The ten gluten-sensitive target organs

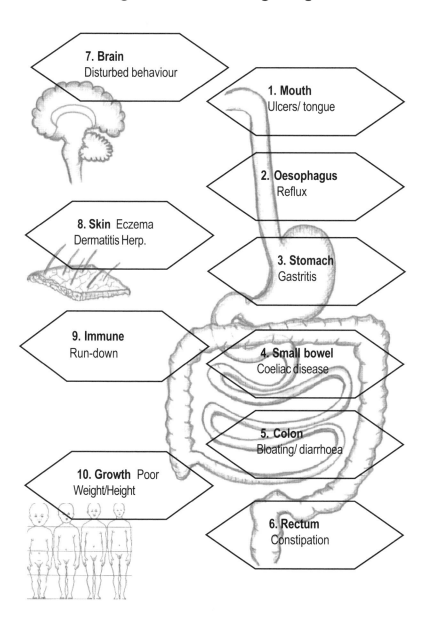

7. Brain
Disturbed behaviour

1. Mouth
Ulcers/ tongue

2. Oesophagus
Reflux

8. Skin Eczema
Dermatitis Herp.

3. Stomach
Gastritis

9. Immune
Run-down

4. Small bowel
Coeliac disease

5. Colon
Bloating/ diarrhoea

10. Growth Poor
Weight/Height

6. Rectum
Constipation

Do you need a blood test?

Yes! You must get some blood tests! If you have symptoms that suggest that you could be gluten-sensitive, the first step is to arrange your blood test with your regular general practitioner. It is very important to have these tests *before* you go gluten-free. We recommend these tests:

☐ **IgG-gliadin** (also called IgG anti-gliadin antibody)

☐ **IgA-gliadin** (also called IgA anti-gliadin antibody)

☐ **ttG antibody** (also called IgA tissue transglutaminase) *or* **EMA** (endomesial antibody)

☐ **Total IgA immunoglobulin levels**
    (looking for deficiency in your IgA antibody production)

☐ **Ferritin** (this is a measure of your iron stores)

☐ **Hb** (Haemoglobin to check for anaemia)

☐ **CRP** (C Reactive-Protein to look for inflammation)

Blood tests are essential before going gluten-free

Can you explain about these blood tests?

Once you have had your blood tests, you will want to know what they mean. Currently, these tests are often misinterpreted. In particular, the IgG-gliadin levels are often dismissed as being meaningless. If you need help with the interpretation of your blood tests, then follow these steps:

1. Get your blood tests and get a copy of these results.
2. Go to the webpage **www.doctorgluten.com**
3. Then, at **Blood Test Results** enter your test results
    (http://www.doctorgluten.com/bloodresults.htm)
4. You will be sent an interpretation of your blood test results with suggestions of what action you should take.

Is coeliac disease the same as gluten-sensitivity?

No! They are not the same. There is an important distinction.

Coeliac disease is a *gastrointestinal* disease of the small bowel which is caused by toxic damage of gluten from your diet. It is also called "gluten-sensitive enteropathy". It is diagnosed if there is tissue damage. This damage is best demonstrated by a small bowel biopsy (by endoscopy). The tissue damage is strongly associated with a positive EMA or tTG antibody test. This gut damage can be fully reversed by a gluten-free diet.

Gluten-sensitivity is a much wider set of problems: the ten target organs are affected – it includes coeliac disease. You are gluten-sensitive if you have symptoms which are provoked by eating gluten. This is usually associated with elevated IgG-gliadin and/or IgA-gliadin antibody levels. This newer concept has led to a major revision in diagnosis and management. The blood tests for gluten-sensitivity have only been available over the last ten years. This has greatly increased the ability to diagnose people with coeliac disease and now gluten-sensitivity.

Symptoms disappear on a gluten-free diet

tTG antibody (an IgA tissue transglutaminase antibody)
The tTG antibody is a specific antibody which is a very sensitive indicator of gut damage. Let me repeat the importance of the tTG result. If you have high tTG antibody test, this indicates that you might have significant small bowel damage – you might have coeliac disease. You should have a confirmatory small bowel biopsy (by endoscopy) *prior* to going gluten-free. You will need to discuss this with your doctor.

13

The gluten-sensitive logo

Hundreds of thousands of people are gluten-sensitive. These people desperately want to *easily* recognise foods that are safe for them to eat. They want to readily identify foods that are gluten-free.

An easily recognised symbol on all suitable food products would solve many of their problems. We have designed a logo to be used on food products which can rapidly identify foods that are safe for gluten-sensitive people to eat.

Safe food for
gluten-sensitive people

This logo has the following elements:
o   A **knife & fork** to show that the symbol deals with food.
o   A **plate**, to show that the symbol deals with meals.
o   An **ear of grain** which symbolises wheat, barley and rye.
o   A **"ban"** symbol to clearly show that the food is gluten-free (ie. contains no gluten).

This is the new international symbol for all products which are safe for those people who are gluten-sensitive. This logo is protected by international copyright.

Criteria and permission for use of this logo on your product can be specifically requested from logo@doctorgluten.com

The best lunch and snack ideas to stay gluten-free

Fresh Fruit

Fruit is one of the mainstays of gluten-free foods. Fresh fruit and dried fruit is nutritious and full of the important vitamins and antioxidants that will keep you healthy. Experiment by mixes of different fruits to give new flavours and textures.

Fresh

Apples	Pears	Bananas
Oranges	Mandarins	Tamarillo
Apricots	Peaches	Nectarines
Rock Melon	Water Melon	Kiwifruit
Grapefruit	Pineapple	Grapes
Strawberries	Raspberries	Boysenberries
Blackcurrants	Blueberries	Cherries
Plums		

Dried

Figs	Apricots	Raisins
Dates	Sultanas	Bananas
Prunes	Crystallised ginger	

Make up fruit kebabs for lunches. Add chunks of various vegetables, dipped in lemon juice and sugar that has been mixed together to keep the colour. Delicious and mouthwatering!

Melon and tomato salad – savoury and sweet mix

1	medium sized melon
500g	tomatoes
1 large	cucumber
1 Tbspn	chopped parsley
1 tsp	chopped mint and chives (heaped)

Cut melon in half, remove seeds and scoop out flesh with melon scoop or cut into cubes. Skin and quarter tomatoes, squeeze out seeds and remove core. Cut smaller if tomatoes are large. Peel the cucumber, and cut into small cubes like the melon. Sprinkle lightly with salt, cover with a plate and let stand for 30 minutes. Drain any liquid and rinse cubes with cold water.

Mix the following dressing together:

2 Tbspns	wine vinegar
6 Tbspns	salad oil.
castor sugar	
salt and pepper	

Mix fruit and vegetables together in a deep bowl, pour over dressing and chill for 2–3 hours. Before serving mix in herbs.

Mint and orange salad

    2 large   oranges
    1 Tbspn chopped mint
    1 Tbspn vinegar
    2 Tbspns olive oil

Peel two large oranges with a vegetable knife and then cut up into cubes. Mix a small bunch of fresh chopped mint with the orange cubes. Toss in the vinegar and olive oil.

Variation: Use grapefruit instead of oranges for a nice change or mix both together.

Apple salad

    1   red skinned apple
    1   green skinned apple
    1   pear
    ½ cup   finely chopped celery
    2 Tbspns finely chopped walnuts
    2 Tbspns polyunsaturated oil
    1 Tbspn   spiced vinegar
    ½ tsp   dried mustard

Cut the unpeeled apples and pear into small cubes. Mix together with the celery and walnuts. Blend the oil, vinegar and mustard together. Pour dressing over apple mixture.

Makes enough for 4 servings.

Children's packed lunches

Five days of lunch box ideas

Here are some great suggestions for what you can pack for your child's school lunch.

Ensure that you pack all items in nice containers so they will remain fresh and won't spoil. Wrap muffins and sandwiches in cling wrap and put in a container that just fits them.

Make salads in their own containers. A small cooler bag to take to and from school or work will help keep the food fresh, especially in the summer months. Cut fruit into small pieces.

Here is some suggestions of packed lunch ideas for a week:

Day One
>   Gluten-free muffins (see Muffin section)
>   Melon salad
>   Banana and orange
>   Popcorn and packet of raisins
>   Pottle of yoghurt
>   Piece of slice, biscuit or cake.

Day Two
>   Sandwiches (see sandwich section)
>   Fresh fruit i.e.: strawberries, apple, grapes
>   Rice crackers with a dip in a separate container
>   Packet of potato chips
>   Dried apricots
>   Piece of slice or cake.

Day Three
> Hard boiled egg
> Cold gluten free sausages and sauce
> Orange and mint salad
> Dates and figs
> Fruit jelly and pineapple or banana
> Piece of slice, biscuit or cake.

Day Four
> Sushi made with avocado, red pepper and/or cucumber
> A pottle of yogurt
> Corn chips and a dip
> Packet of raisins
> Apple or pear
> Piece of slice or cake.

Day Five
> Sandwiches
> Rice crackers and dip
> Banana and mandarins
> Packet of chips
> Dried apricots
> Piece of slice or cake.

Here are other things that you can pack for your child's school lunch:

o   Gluten-free scones or muffins.
o   Small packets of dried fruit such as: raisins, dried apricots, pears, peaches, apples or prunes.
o   Gluten-free potato chips and or mixed nuts (avoid dry roasted nuts as these may contain gluten).
o   Raw carrot or cucumber sticks.
o   Rice salad, gluten-free pasta salad, tuna salad, bean salad, potato salad or salads that your child likes.
o   Gluten-free soups (home-made) – best for when you are at home but can be taken in a flask.
o   Hard boiled eggs.
o   Fresh fruit.
o   Fresh fruit salad.
o   Fresh fruit jelly (set in small containers).
o   Plain or fruit flavoured fromage frais, natural yoghurt with fresh fruit added.
o   Drinks, unsweetened fruit juices, milk, home-made smoothies, water.
o   Rice crackers and toppings and/or dips.
o   Gluten-free bread made into sandwiches.
o   Small mini pizzas.
o   Cold gluten-free sausages.
o   Tortilla chips.

Some of these ideas can be made in advance and kept in containers in the fridge. Being more organised can make lunch ideas easy and quick.

Eggs and vegetables

Eggs are very good for lunches. You can do the following:

Hard boiled egg in the shell
Hard boil an egg. Draw a smiley face on it or shell it ready to eat. Wrap in cling wrap to keep fresh.

Stuffed hard boiled eggs
Shell the eggs.   Cut in half and then take the yolk out. In a separate bowl mash the yolk with a little mixed yoghurt and curry powder. Put back into the egg.
Half an egg can be used one day and the other the next day.

Baked eggs on rice
　　　6 Tbspns　　rice
　　　2 Tbspns　　melted butter
　　　1½ cups　　stock
　　　1 large　　　onion
　　　grated cheese
　　　salt and pepper
　　　As many eggs as required

Wash and dry rice and brown with onion in butter.
Add stock, mix well and turn into buttered casserole.
Cover and bake in moderate oven 180°C for about 40 minutes.
Uncover, make indentations in the rice and slip in whole eggs.
Sprinkle with grated cheese, salt and pepper.
Return to the oven and bake until eggs are set.

Vegetables and dipping sauces

Let your imagination go wild – think of all the vegetables that can be chopped up into bite size pieces to be dipped in tasty dips. For example:

Asparagus – lightly blanched
Broccoli   Carrots   Cauliflower
Celery   Cucumber   Gherkins
Green beans – lightly blanched
Mushrooms – small or sliced
Radishes
Small cobs of corn
Tomatoes – baby ones or sliced
Potato wedges with tomato dip
Partly cook whole potatoes in the oven (or you can use prepackaged frozen ones). Cut into wedges.

Make a dipping sauce with the following:

750mls   plain yoghurt
2 Tbspns   chilli sauce
500g ripe tomatoes, finely chopped
2 Tbspns   fresh coriander, finely chopped
75g roasted salted peanuts, finely chopped
2 Tbspns   oil
1 tsp   black mustard seeds
½ tsp   cumin seeds
pinch chilli powder
pinch ground turmeric

In a bowl combine yoghurt, chilli sauce, chopped tomatoes, coriander and peanuts. Heat oil in a small frying pan. Add the chilli powder, turmeric, mustard seeds and cumin seeds. Cover and cook for a few seconds until the seeds begin to crackle and pop.

Remove from the heat and scrape the spices over the yoghurt mixture. Fold to combine. Garnish with fresh chopped tomatoes, coriander and serve with the potatoes.

Variation: For a change try Kumara wedges.

Home-made baked beans

½ Tbspn	olive oil
1 small	onion, finely chopped
80g	smoky bacon, finely chopped
20g	brown sugar
1 Tbspn	red wine vinegar
200g	tinned tomatoes, pureed
3 tsps	worcester sauce
400g	tin white beans, drained and rinsed

Heat the oil in a deep saucepan, fry the onion and bacon until starting to brown. Add the sugar, stir and cook until caramelised. Add the vinegar and boil for one minute to reduce the liquid. Stir in the tomatoes and simmer for 10–15 minutes.

Add the Worcester sauce and white beans, stir and simmer for a further 5–10 minutes.

Baked potatoes

Bake potatoes in a hot oven until tops are golden brown. Cut in half and put in your favourite fillings – such as:

Cheese, tomatoes, creamed corn, chopped onion, bacon (gluten free) and parsley.

A suggested filling for 4 pre-cooked potatoes:

Ricotta cheese and chives – 30g ricotta cheese, 2 tsps finely chopped chives, black pepper to taste, 1 egg white.

Vegetable fritters

2	medium	potatoes, peeled
1	medium	carrot, peeled
2	medium	zucchini
120g		sweet potato, peeled
1		small leek
2 Tbspns		GF flour
3		eggs, lightly beaten

oil for frying

Finely grate, potatoes, carrot, zucchini and sweet potato.
Finely slice leek (white part only).
Cup small handfuls of grated vegetables in both hands and squeeze out as much excess moisture as possible. Place into a large mixing bowl with leek and combine well.

Sprinkle flour over vegetables and combine. Add eggs and mix well. Heat about 5mm of oil in a frying pan and drop ¼ cup of mixture into neat piles. Use a fork to gently form mixture into a 10cm round. Fry 2-3 minutes until golden brown and crispy. Drain on paper towel. Keep warm. Repeat with rest of mixture.

Variation: you can make tomato salsa or tomato sauce with these fritters or dipping sauce.

Potato puffs

1½ cups	cooked mashed potato
3 Tbspns	milk
2 Tbspns	melted butter
60g	grated cheese (¾ cup)
2 eggs,	separated
½ tsp	paprika
1 Tbspn	chopped parsley
	or finely chopped green pepper
1 small onion (grated)	
1 tsp salt	

Beat mashed potatoes with milk and butter. Add cheese and egg yolks. Combine with other ingredients. Fold in stiffly beaten egg whites. Drop in small mounds onto a greased baking tray and bake 20 minutes at 180⁰C – until nicely browned.

Nutty corn fritters

1 cup	corn kernels
1 cup	roasted peanuts
3	spring onions, chopped
2 tsps	grated fresh ginger
1 clove	garlic crushed
1 tsp	ground cumin
1 egg	lightly beaten
2 Tbspns	rice flour
½ cup	peanut oil

Put corn, peanuts, spring onions, ginger, garlic, and cumin in a food process and process until finely chopped and slightly mushy. Transfer to a bowl. Add egg and rice flour, mix well. Heat oil in pan, put spoonfuls of mixture into pan and flatten with the back of the spoon. Cook over medium heat until golden brown on both sides. Drain on absorbent paper.

Rice

Spicy wild rice salad

400g	wild rice blend
2 Tbspns	vegetable oil
2	onions cut into thin wedges
1 tsp	ground cumin
½ tsp	ground cinnamon
¼ tsp	ground cloves
¼ tsp	ground ginger
2	carrots, thinly sliced
1 tsp	honey
2	oranges, segmented
85g	pistachios, toasted and roughly chopped
85g	raisins
55g	flaked almonds, toasted
3	spring onions sliced
3 Tbspns	chopped fresh dill

Cook rice in boiling water until tender. Drain well and set aside to cool. Heat oil in nonstick frying pan over a medium heat.

Add onions, cumin, cinnamon, cloves and ginger and cook, stirring for 10 minutes or until onions are soft and slightly caramelised. Add carrots and cook until tender. Stir in honey, then remove from heat and cool slightly. Place rice, carrot mixture, oranges, pistachios, raisins, almonds, spring onions and dill in a bowl and toss to combine.

To make dressing:

1 tsp	Dijon mustard
½ cup	olive oil
¼ cup	orange juice
1 Tbspn	red wine vinegar

Place mustard, oil, orange juice and vinegar in a bowl and whisk to combine. Pour over salad and toss.

Sushi

3 sheets	seaweed for sushi
500g	cooked sushi rice

Make sushi with the following fillings:

	carrot sticks, blanched
1 bunch	watercress, blanched
1 Tbspn	pickle
3 small	spring onions
	cucumber strips

Dampen the hands and press the rice over the seaweed to an even thickness of 0.5cm. Keep the rice in from the edges, especially the faraway edge. Press in the vegetables or pickles. Roll up mat like a swiss roll. Squeeze the roll to firm.
Cut into 2.5cm rounds.

Sushi-zu vinegar

Mix together:

1 Tbspn	sugar
1 tsp	salt
¼ cup	sherry *or* rice wine
¼ cup	rice vinegar

Sushi toasted rice balls

¾ cup	sushi-zu rice vinegar
3 cups	cooked sushi-style rice
2 Tbspns	black sesame seeds
2 Tbspns	toasted sesame seeds

Mix the vinegar through the warm sushi rice, toss well and leave to cool.

Mix the black and toasted sesame seeds on a tray and roll the sticky rice balls in the sesame seeds. Cover with plastic wrap and chill until required. Serve with soy sauce (gluten-free) mixed if desired with a little wasabi.

Sesame seed and rice parcels

8–10	large cabbage leaves or Chinese leaves
280g	brown rice, cooked.
1 Tbpn	sesame seeds
1 tsp	celery seeds
½ tsp	oregano
1 Tbspn	tahini sesame cream (optional
1 Tbspn	GF soy sauce

Steam the greens gently until tender.
Mix the rice with the rest of the ingredients and spoon onto the leaves.
Wrap up each leaf and place in an ovenproof dish, with the folds downwards so that they do not unwrap. Dot with butter or vegetable oil.
Cover and bake for 20 minutes at 180⁰C.

Meat

Chicken marinate

Marinate chicken drums in your favourite mix, grill and have cold in the lunch box.

A good chicken marinate is:

1 Tbspn	honey
2 tsps	GF soy sauce
1 Tbspn	sesame seeds

Remove skin from chicken, mix honey and GF soy sauce together, spread over chicken, sprinkle with sesame seeds. Bake 200⁰C for 20–25 minutes or until golden brown.

Caramelised chicken wings

12 chicken wings (or similar)	
2 Tbspns	peanut oil
3 cloves	garlic, crushed
1Tbspn	chopped fresh ginger
1Tbspn	fish sauce
1Tbspn	GF soy sauce
¼ cup	(60mls) honey

Cut wings in half at joint and discard tip. Heat oil in large pan, stir-fry garlic, ginger and chicken for 5 minutes. Stir in sauces and honey, cook, covered stirring occasionally (15 minutes) or until chicken is tender and brown.

Satay chicken skewers

(soak skewers in cold water for several hours to stop them from scorching when cooking)

12	chicken thigh fillets
1 cup	chicken stock
½ cup	crunchy peanut butter
¼ cup	mild sweet chilli sauce
1 Tbspn	lime juice
¼ cup	coconut milk
2 tsps	brown sugar

Cut each fillet into 12 cubes, thread on 12 skewers, cook skewers in batches, in heated oiled pan or grill on barbecue until tender.

Combine remaining ingredients in medium pan, stir over heat for about 5 minutes or until sauce thickens. Serve sauce over chicken skewers.

Other meat ideas:

o   A little chicken pate with rice crackers.

o   Slice finely beef, ham, lamb.

o   Make kebabs, beef, lamb chicken. Put on skewers and grill until cooked. Great in lunches for a change.

Add vegetables between meat for new taste experiences.

Bacon and zucchini slice

600g	zucchini, coarsely grated
6 slices	lean GF bacon, finely chopped
2 medium	onion, sliced finely
6	eggs
½ cup	cream *or* sour cream
½ cup	grated cheese
2 Tbpns	chopped parsley

Beat eggs until light and fluffy. Then combine all of the other ingredient. Mix until well combined. Put into a greased baking dish or pie dish. Bake at 180°C for 40 minutes. It should be golden brown.

Cut into slices when cool. Can wrap in glad wrap for a nice change for lunch.

Gluten-free sandwich ideas

Natalie's Brown Bread

Place into a bowl

2 cups	warm water, or milk
1¼ tsps	yeast
1 Tbspn	brown sugar
1	egg
3 Tbspns	oil

approx. 500gms *Healtheries* bread mix;
　　　　　or half bread mix and half baking mix
1 heaped Tbspn coarse cornmeal
1 heaped Tbspn fine cornmeal *or* rice flour
1 heaped Tbspn ground linseed
1 heaped Tbspn sunflower seeds
1 heaped Tbspn pumpkin seeds [optional]
1 tsp　　　guar gum

Mix ingredients gently together.
Scrape the firmish mixture into bread maker 'bucket.

Cook on rapid programme with dark crust.
(Best suited for Breville Bread maker. Some other bread makers
might use 'basic' programme for best results).

If bread sinks in centre it may be too moist at the start.

Sandwich combinations

o Grated carrot, chopped celery and sliced tomato
o Sliced tomato and low fat cheese slices
o Leftover fish, flaked and chopped with chives
o Chicken, thinly sliced pineapple
o Leftover curried vegetables
o Grated carrot, low fat cheese slices, raisins

o Mashed or sliced banana and raisins
o Thinly sliced apple, lemon juice and chopped dates
o Apple spread and sultanas
o Apple spread, grated apple and cinnamon
o Apricot and fruit spread, finely chopped walnuts

Tomato cheese filling

2 tsps tomato puree, ½ tsp dry basil, ¼ tsp black pepper, 1 tomato chopped, peeled and seeded, 1 egg white. Mix together. Sprinkle with finely grated cheese.

Big dagwood sandwich

Spread bread with date and apple chutney. Spread over chopped cooked chicken. Season to taste. Top with second piece of bread, spread with cottage cheese, slices of tomato, onion slices, cucumber slices, alfalfa sprouts and season with black pepper. Top with third piece of bread.

Apple filling

¼ cup	finely grated cheese
1 small	apple grated
¼ tsp	Dijon mustard

Mix together and spread on bread.

Celery and walnut filling

30g	ricotta cheese
4 Tbspns	finely chopped celery
2 Tbspns	finely chopped walnuts and black pepper

Mix together and spread on bread.

Apple Spread

220g	dried apples
3 cups	unsweetened pineapple juice
½	lemon
2 tsps	lemon rind
2 tsps	cinnamon

Combine all ingredients in a large saucepan and simmer over gentle heat until apples are soft. Puree the mixture in a blender and pour into sterilised jar.
When cool, seal and store in the fridge.

Apricot fruit spread

125g	apricots
90g	dried apples
60g	raisins
3½ cups	unsweetened orange juice

Combine all ingredients in a large saucepan and simmer over gentle heat until fruit is soft. Puree in a blender and pour into sterilised jar. When cool, seal and store in the fridge.

More lunch box ideas

Put together a selection of the following to make your lunch box more interesting:

o   Steamed chicken drumsticks. Have with a green salad made from lettuce (different varieties), grated carrot and cubes of tasty cheese. Sprinkle a light vinaigrette dressing over salad

o   Celery and rice crackers with cottage cheese, chopped celery, chopped chicken, walnuts. Add to this fresh fruit, a salad made from cold cooked rice, cashew nuts and sultanas

o   Pack a tomato, apple cucumber, small bits of lettuce, chunks of low fat cheese, sticks of celery. Two pieces of fresh fruit and a pottle of yoghurt

o   Pack cottage cheese or nonfat yoghurt with an apple, an orange and a banana. Have rice crackers and cold cooked chicken pieces

o   Gluten free cherrios and cold sausages are good for lunches. Have with slices of buttered Gluten free bread. Add a fresh fruit salad

o   Pre-prepared snack food from the supermarket

o   Corn chips *or* Kettle style chips. Have these with a nice dip or two dips. A kebab made with cheese, celery and tomato

o   Popcorn – microwave popcorn, flavour of choice. Put in small pottles for school lunches o   Make small individual jellies (ensure they are gluten-free), mix in fruit and set

o   Add fresh fruit to have with jellies. Add yoghurt as well. Can sprinkle GF muesli for a change or have in a separate container

Kebab snacks

1 wooden skewer thread with the following:
    cheese chunks
    celery chunks
    carrot chunks
    pineapple wedges
    grapes
    radish chunks
    tomato chunks

Wrap in glad wrap for safe handling. Nice for a change in the lunch box.

Pizza, dips and wraps

Pizza base, quick and easy

¼ cup	milk
2 large	eggs
¹/3 cup	cornstarch
²/3 cup	rice flour
¼ tsp	xanthan gum
1 tsp	salt
¼ cup	butter, melted

Beat the milk and eggs together. Add the flours, xanthan gum and salt. Mix in melted butter. Spread with a spatula into a round circle about 1cm thick on a round pizza pan, leaving a thicker crust around the outside of the circle to keep the cause and cheese from running out. Spread sauce evenly over the unbaked crust and top with your favourite toppings. Bake in a preheated oven 200⁰C for about 25 minutes.

Pizza sauce topping

1 tin	chopped tomatoes
¼ tsp	crushed oregano leaves
½ tsp	dried crushed basil
2 Tbspns	sugar, or to taste
¼ tsp	crushed garlic

Mix altogether, then spread over pizza base.
Top with your choice of toppings. For example:
grated mozzarella cheese
or gluten-free sausage chopped small.
or olives, mushrooms, chicken, bacon, ham, prawns.

Gluten-free pizza base – thin crust
(Courtesy Bakels)

2 cups	*Bakels Gluten Free Pastry Mix*
1 tsp	sugar
¾ cup	water
1 tsp	salt
1 tsp	Dry Active Yeast
1	egg
2 Tbspns	olive oil

Place *Bakels Gluten Free Pastry Mix*, salt, sugar and dry active yeast into a large mixing bowl. In a jug mix together water, egg and olive oil and pour into dry mix. Mix together until dough forms.

Remove from bowl and kneed well for a few minutes. Shape dough into a ball, place in a bowel and cover with a cloth.

Let sit in a warm place for 1–1½ hours. Punch down and roll out to fit pizza pan.

Top with desired toppings and bake at 210ºC for 20–25 minutes.

Roast vegetable pizza
Use left-over vegetables, roasted and cut into pieces and put on the sauce.

Potato pan pizza
(Courtesy of Healtheries)

1 cup	*Simple Baking Mix*
100g	(approx. 1 large) cooked potato, mashed
50g	softened butter
½ tsp	dried marjoram or preferred herb

Topping

2 medium	tomatoes, chopped
2 or 3	rashers bacon, chopped
1	green pepper, chopped
1 cup	chopped mushrooms
½ tsp	dried basil
1 cup	cooked cubed potato
½ tsp	dried marjoram
2 cups	grated cheddar cheese
extra cheese (optional)	

Preheat oven to 200⁰C. In a processor, mix together the baking mix, potato, butter and marjoram. Press into a greased loose-bottom cake tin.

Place the topping ingredients into a bowl and mix evenly together. Spread over the base and press down firmly. Add extra cheese if desired.

Bake for 25–30 minutes, until the base is cooked and the topping golden. Serves 2.

Hummus

300g	can chick peas or 1 cup cooked chick peas
3 Tbspns	tahini
¼ cup	lemon juice
1 glove	garlic
¼ cup	oil

Drain chick peas. Place chick peas, tahini and lemon juice in the bowl of a food processor or blender. Crush and peel garlic. Add to peas. Process until chick peas are chopped. Gradually add oil down the feed tube and process until mixture is smooth and the required consistency for use.

Easy guacamole

1 ripe	avocado, peeled
Small pinch	chilli powder
1½–2 Tbspns	olive oil
1–2 Tbspns	lemon juice
1	small onion, finely chopped
pinch of salt	

Mash avocado with chilli powder, olive oil and lemon juice. Salt to taste. Fold in onion and garnish with slices of lemon. Serve.

Salsa and avocado

Make a fresh salsa with diced ripe tomatoes, roasted red capsicum, a little chopped red onion, chopped parsley and diced avocado. Season with salt and pepper.

Muffins, bars and slices

Corn and feta muffins
(Courtesy of Healtheries)

3 cups	*Simple Baking Mix*
4 tsps	baking powder
½ tsp	salt
¼ tsp	pepper
300g can	kernel corn, drained
	or 1 cup drained kernel corn
150g	feta cheese, finely crumbled
2	spring onions, finely sliced
1½cups	milk
1/3 cup	vegetable oil
2	eggs

Preheat oven to 200°C. Grease 12 deep muffin tins. Combine Bread Mix, baking powder, salt and pepper in a large bowl. Stir in corn, feta and spring onions.

Whisk together milk, oil and eggs. Pour liquid ingredients over dry ingredients. Mix lightly until ingredients are just combined. Do not over mix.

Divide mixture between prepared tins. Brush with a little milk and egg. Bake for 15-20 minutes until golden. Stand for 5 minutes before removing from tins.

Zucchini (courgette) muffins

$1/3$ cup	sugar
2	eggs
3 Tbspns	vegetable oil
1 cup	GF flour mix
1 tsp	baking powder
¾ tsp	salt
½ tsp	baking soda
¼ tsp	cinnamon
¼ tsp	nutmeg
1 cup	grated zucchini
¼ cup	raisins
¼ cup	chopped walnuts

Beat together sugar, eggs and oil. Combine the flour, baking powder, salt, baking soda, cinnamon, and nutmeg. Stir these into the sugar mixture. The mixture will seem dry.

Stir in the zucchini, raisins and nuts. Grease muffin tins and spoon mixture ¾ full. Bake in a hot oven 200°C for 20 minutes. Makes 10–12.

Savoury muffins

(Courtesy Bakels)

70g	butter, melted
3	eggs
1¼ cups	milk
2 tsps	baking powder
2½ cups	*Bakels Gluten Free Baking Mix*
1 tsp	salt
1	red onion, chopped finely
1	green pepper, chopped into cubes
1 cup	cheese
pinch of pepper	

Melt butter and let cool slightly. Mix eggs and milk together and add to butter. Sift *Bakels Gluten Free Baking Mix*, baking powder, salt and pepper into a bowl, add onion, green pepper and cheese. Combine then add liquid. Mix well.

Spoon mixture into well greased muffin tray. Top with cheese if desired.
Bake at 190⁰C for 15–20 minutes or until golden.

Leave in tin for 10 minutes before turning onto a cooling rack. Makes approximately 10–12.

Alternatively substitute green pepper for ham or bacon.

Spicy carrot muffins

¼ cup	brown sugar
½ cup	rice bran
2	eggs
3 Tbspns	vegetable oil
1½ cups	GF flour mix
4 tsp	GF baking powder
¾ tsp	salt
¾ tsp	baking soda
1 tsp	cinnamon
¼ tsp	nutmeg
1 cup	grated carrots
2/3 cup	orange juice
1/3 cup	raisins
¼ cup	vegetable oil

In a large bowl combine flour, bran, cinnamon, baking soda, baking powder, and nutmeg. Mix well.

Combine carrots, orange juice, raisins, oil, brown sugar, and eggs.

Add to dry mixture mixing until dry ingredients are moistened. Grease 10 muffin pans *or* line with patty pans (liners). Fill about ¾ full of mixture. Let stand for 5 minutes.

Bake at 200⁰C for 20–25 minutes *(can be used for dessert as well)*.

Katherine's spiced fruit muffins
(wheat, gluten, dairy and egg free)

½ cup	rice flour
1 cup	fine rolled oats
2 tsps	mixed spice
½ tsp	baking soda
½ cup	buckwheat flour
¾ cup	brown sugar
2 tsps	cinnamon
½ tsp	salt
75g	dairy free spread
1 tsp	*Orgran* egg replacer mixed with 2 Tbspn of water
1	410 gram tin of fruit drained and chopped (for example, peaches, pears *or* apricots)
¾–1 cup	soy or rice milk

Sieve flours and mix dry ingredients into a large mixing bowl. Ensure brown sugar and rolled oats are well mixed with no large lumps. Melt the dairy free spread until liquid, mix in the egg replacer, fruit, and ¾ cup of rice or soy milk.

Add the fruit and liquid mixture to the dry ingredients. Take care not to over mix. Use some or all of the extra ¼ cup of soy or rice milk as necessary.

Use some dairy free spread to grease 12 medium-sized muffin pan. Put muffin mix into this equally. Bake at 200⁰C for approx 12 minutes or until springy. Stand for 5 minutes before removing from pan and cooling on a rack.

Raspberry-lemon muffins
(Courtesy of Healtheries)

3 level cups	*Simple Baking Mix*
1 cup	milk
¼ cup	cooking oil
2	eggs, lightly beaten
1 tsp	vanilla essence
2 tsps	grated lemon peel
1¼ cups	raspberries (frozen or fresh)

Glaze
2 Tbspns	sugar
2 Tbspns	lemon juice

Preheat oven to 200⁰C and grease a 12 cup muffin tin.
Add the *Healtheries Simple Baking Mix* into a mixing bowl and make a well in the centre.

In a separate bowl, combine the milk, oil, eggs, vanilla essence and lemon peel and pour into the well of the flour mixture. Stir until the ingredients are moistened then add the raspberries and stir in gently.

Spoon dough into muffin tins and bake for 20–25 minutes.
While muffins are baking prepare the glaze by combining the lemon juice and sugar. Lemon juice may need to be warmed to completely dissolve the sugar.

Remove from oven and drizzle glaze over the warm muffins.

Ginger friands

175g	melted butter (unsalted)
1 cup	ground almonds
½ cup	GF baking mix
2 tsps	ground ginger
2 Tbspns	golden syrup
1½ cups	icing sugar
6	egg whites (slightly beaten)

Preheat oven to 180⁰C. Combine all ingredients, adding egg white last. Just combine, do not over mix. Fill lightly greased friand tins to ¾ with the mixture. Bake in oven for 20 minutes until golden. Makes 10.

Raisin puffs (makes 24)

2 cups	soy flour
4 tsps	GF baking powder
1 cup	chopped raisins
2 tsps	orange or lemon rind
1 Tbspn	honey or golden syrup
1–1½ cups	skimmed milk
60g	finely minced dried apple

Sift four and baking powder together twice. Add raisins, rind, honey or golden syrup. Stir, adding the milk. The mixture should be slightly sticky. Add apples. Place teaspoons of mixture into paper patties and place on a baking tray. Bake in a moderate oven 170⁰C for 15 minutes or until tops are golden brown. Break open and fill with apple spread or apricot and fruit spread.

Peanut butter bars (no baking required)

5 cups	GF puffed or crisped rice cereal
1 cup	raisins
1 cup	dark corn syrup
1 cup	chunky peanut butter
1 cup	sugar

In a large bowl, mix the rice cereal and raisins together. Set aside whit you heat the syrup, peanut butter and sugar in a saucepan over a low heat until it bubbles. (You can use the microwave as well).

Pour the hot syrup over the rice cereal and raisins and blend together. Press the mixture into a buttered square pan.
Cut into squares when cool. Makes 20 6cm bars.

Peanut butter biscuits

1 cup	peanut butter
1 cup	caster sugar
1 egg	lightly beaten

Combine all ingredients in medium bowl, stir until combined. Roll rounded teaspoons of mixture into balls. Place biscuits onto greased oven trays, about 5cm apart, flatten slightly with a fork.

Bake in moderate oven for about 15 minutes or until golden brown. Stand biscuits 5 minutes, turn onto wire rack to cool. Makes about 30.

Easy five-cup slice

1 cup	sultanas
1 cup	dark chocolate bits
1 cup	unsalted roasted peanuts
1 cup	desiccated coconut
1 cup	sweetened condensed milk
50g	dark chocolate, melted

Line 20cm x 30cm lamington pan with baking paper, extending paper 2cm over edge of long sides of pan.
Sprinkle pan with sultans, cock bits, peanuts and coconut.
Drizzle with condensed milk.

Bake, covered in a moderately hot oven for 20 minutes. Reduce heat to moderate. Uncover and bake 15 minutes. Cool in pan.
Drizzle melted chocolate over slice. Leave to set before cutting.

Coconut and lime macaroons

2 cups	desiccated coconut
½ cup	sugar
2	egg whites
1 Tbspn	shredded lime zest

Preheat oven to 180⁰C. Place the egg whites, coconut, sugar and zest into a bowl and mix well to combine. Roll the mixture into small balls, place on a lined baking tray and flatten slightly.
Bake for 10–15 minutes until golden, but not too brown.

Apricot and almond health bars

½ cup	chopped apricots
¼ cup	orange juice
2 Tbspns	honey
½ cup	skim milk powder
¼ cup	whole almonds roughly chopped
1 Tbspn	toasted sesame seeds
1 tsp	grated orange rind
½ cup	sultanas or currants
¼ cup	coconut

extra raw toasted coconut

Place apricots, orange juice and honey in a saucepan and simmer over low heat for 10 minutes or until apricots are tender. Do not drain. Blend in skim milk powder, add almonds, sesame seeds, grated orange rind, sultanas and coconut. Mix well and leave to cool slightly.

Roll mixture into a log shape and roll in toasted coconut. Roll up in foil and keep in the fridge. Cut into slices and store in a jar or wrap each individual piece in foil for school lunches.

Tasty cheese sticks

250g	cheddar cheese
2 Tbspns	butter or margarine
1 large	egg
½ tsp	salt
1/8 tsp	ground pepper
¾ cup	rice flour
¼ cup	potato starch flour
1 tsp	xanthan gum

Grate the cheese (2 cups). Set aside. Put butter into bowl and beat until creamy. Add, egg, salt and pepper. Beat until blended. Beat in cheese a third at a time until combined. Stir in flours and xanthan gum until thoroughly blended. Work the dough into a ball. If dough does not stick together, add cold water 1 tablespoon at a time until a ball can be formed.

Divide dough, rolling half at a time between sheets of wax paper for form a rectangle about 1cm thick. Cut with pastry wheel into long strips 1.2cm x 15cm and place on baking sheets. Bake in oven at 200°C for 6–8 minutes, until dark golden. Let cool on racks and store airtight for up to a week. Should make around 50 cheese sticks.

Pikelets
(Courtesy Bakels)

2 cups	*Bakels Gluten Free Baking Mix*
2	eggs
2 tsps	baking powder
½ tsp	salt
½ cup	sugar
1¹/3 cups	milk

Sift *Bakels Gluten Free Baking mix*, baking powder, and salt into a bowl. Combine eggs, sugar and milk. Add to the sifted ingredients and mix until a smooth batter. Deposit desired quantities onto a greased frying pan or hot plate. Turn pikelets over when bubbles start bursting on the top of the pikelet.

Cook until golden brown. Makes approximately 15–20.

Fabulous pancakes
(Courtesy of Healtheries)

> 1¼ cups of milk & 1¼ tsps white vinegar –
> Mix to make buttermilk
> ¼ cup + 2 Tbspns *Healtheries Ground Millet*
> 2 Tbspns   *Healtheries Fine Ground Linseed*
> ½ tsp   vanilla essence
>   (note: Hansells Vanilla Essence is gluten free)
> 1 Tbspn   oil
> 1   egg lightly beaten
> 1¼ cups   *Healtheries Simple Baking Mix*
> ½ tsp   baking soda (sieved)
>   (note: Hansells baking mix is gluten free)
> ½ tsp   salt

Mix buttermilk, millet, linseed and vanilla essence together.
Let it stand for 10 minutes, stirring occasionally.
Stir in oil and egg.

Combine baking mix, baking soda and salt, stir well.
Add the liquid ingredients to the dry ingredients, stir until smooth.

Spoon about 1/3 of a cup of batter onto a lightly oiled nonstick pan. Cook until pancake tops are covered with bubbles and edges looked cooked. Turn and cool the other side.

These pancakes freeze well. This recipe can also be used to make pikelets. Store Linseed in airtight container in fridge.

Sweet treats

Carob balls

300g	butter
3 Tbspns	carob
2 cups	sultanas
1 cup	currants
1 cup	chopped nuts
4 cups	milk powder
3 Tbspns	golden syrup
2 tsps	cinnamon
1½ cups	dates
½ cup	sesame seeds
1 cup	coconut

Melt together the butter, and golden syrup. Add the carob and cinnamon and mix to a rich smooth syrup.

Add all the dried fruit, but chop the dates first so they are very small. Finally, add the coconut and remove from the heat. Pour in the milk powder cup by cup and beat in well. This becomes harder to do as the mixture becomes stiffer, but aim for a smooth texture without pockets of dry powder.

Press the mixture into a flat greased tin, and top with a little coconut, or alternatively roll into small balls and dip each into a plate of coconut to coat all over. Cool in the fridge.

Stuffed prunes
Use pre-prepared prunes and fill with the following mixture.

½ cup	gluten-free breadcrumbs
1 tsp	lemon juice
1 Tbspn	chopped parsley
pinch of sage	

Fruit leather
1kg Berrycrush

Spread evenly into a foil lined swiss roll tin. Dry in a very slow oven with the door slightly ajar until fruit is dry to touch and without any trace of stickiness.

Cool to room temperature. Peel away foil. Roll "leather" for easy storage.

Cheese walnut balls
125g cream cheese
125g walnut halves
2 rashers bacon

Grill bacon until crisp, crumble until very fine.
Roll cheese into small balls, press a walnut on each side.

Roll in the crumbed bacon until the edges of the cheese are coated. Serve with rice crackers.

Party popcorn

4 cups	plain popped popcorn
6 dried	apricot halves diced
20g	raisins and sultanas
3 tsps	(12 g) sunflower seeds
¼ cup	golden syrup
9 tsps	firmly packed light brown sugar
1 tsp	vanilla essence

In a large bowl combine the popcorn, apricots, raisins, sultanas and sunflower seeds.

In a small saucepan combine the remaining ingredients, set candy thermometer in pan and cook over medium-high heat until thermometer reaches 110⁰C (or cook until a drop of hot mixture spins a 5cm thread when dropped into cold water).

Pour sugar mixture over popcorn mixture and toss quickly to thoroughly coat.

Spray rectangle baking dish with nonstick booking spray, turn popcorn mixture into dish and using back of a spoon, press mixture into the dish.

Let stand until mixture cools (5–10 minutes). Invert onto serving dish and cut into four equal portions.

Gluten-free pantry

Foods that *are* gluten-free

A big part of keeping gluten-free is to know what foods are safe, and what foods might contain gluten. It is a matter of always being vigilant.

If you make a mistake, then that is okay. Accidental gluten now and then will not cause you any long term harm. However, you might feel ill for a few hours or even for a few days.

Errors are learning experiences

A list of some gluten-free foods

o   Amaranth seeds (ground into flour or also makes quinod cereal)
o   Arrowroot (a starch product prepared from a plant)
o   Beverages – cocoa, coffee, tea
o   Buckwheat (a triangular-shaped seed – not from wheat)
o   Chick pea flour (also known as besan flour)
o   Commercially made GF flours & baking mixes
o   Condiments – mustard, olives, plain pickles, salt, pepper
o   Cornmeal (maize) – ground or polenta
o   Dairy products – milk, yoghurt, cheese (unprocessed)
o   Eggs
o   Fish and all seafood. – fresh and unprocessed.
o   Fruit – fresh, canned
o   Gelatin – desserts, jelly
o   Herbs & spices – fresh

- o   *Maize* cornflour
- o   Meat – unprocessed
- o   Millet (a grain widely used in India)
- o   Nuts & seeds – plain
- o   Oils & fats
- o   Popcorn – unflavoured
- o   Poppadums
- o   Potato flour (it is starch with good thickening properties)
- o   Rice – grain, flour, bran
- o   Rice breakfast cereals (malt free)
- o   Rice cakes & crackers (plain)
- o   Rice noodles & pasta
- o   Rice paper – use for wraps
- o   Soya – flour, tofu, milk & yoghurt (GF)
- o   Sugar, jams & honey
- o   Split pea – whole, flour
- o   Spreads – butter, margarine, vegetable oil, shortening
- o   Syrups – golden syrup and maple syrup
- o   Tamari soy sauce
- o   Tapioca (also called cassava)
- o   Vegetables – fresh, tinned
- o   Wine, cider, port, sherry

A complete commercial list of gluten-free foods can be seen on the manufacturer's food database website: **www.mfd.co.nz**

Food additives often do contain gluten

Check if there are any gluten-containing additives. Beware, that many food additives are made from gluten grains. Therefore, these additives will add gluten to your food. This is the most tedious part of gluten-free eating. You will need to avoid all of these. So, check the food labels carefully for the following:

Food additives that *DO* contain gluten

o   Amylases: # 1100 – these enzymes are often produced from malted cereals. They contain traces of gluten.
o   Glutamates: # 620, 621, 622, 623, 624, 625 – are generally gluten-free. But some may be derived from wheat.
o   Starch: # 1400 range (if wheat-based).
o   Maltodextrin – if derived from wheat.
o   Malt extract.
o   Vinegar – if malt based.
o   Soy sauce – which is usually wheat-based.
o   HVP – Hydrolysed Vegetable Protein.
o   HPP – Hydrolysed Plant Protein.

Many food additives *do* contain gluten

Foods that *MAY* contain gluten

o   Baked beans
o   Baking powder
o   Budget brands of ground almonds
o   Canned meats, soups, sauces
o   Cheeses – processed, spreads, blue
o   Chewing gum
o   Chocolate bars, drinks, mixes
o   Coffee substitutes
o   Custard powder
o   Dried soup mixes, sauces, gravy
o   Fizzy drinks
o   Flavoured chips & snacks
o   Fruit flavoured drinks
o   Marshmallows
o   Mayonnaise
o   Mustard powder
o   Peanut butter and nut butters
o   Processed meats – luncheon meats, sausages
o   Pudding mixes
o   Salad dressings

You must read food ingredient labels carefully

o   Scotch eggs
o   Seasoning mixes, stock cubes
o   Soup bases
o   Sour cream
o   Soy sauce
o   Sweets, lollies, candies.

Foods that *DO* contain gluten
These foods are *not* allowed

o   Barley-based foods
o   Rye-based foods
o   Wheat-based foods
>   Bread, bread crumbs, rolls
>   Brewers yeast
>   Biscuits, crackers, cookies
>   Coucous
>   Croissants, donuts, pancakes, flapjacks
>   Malt
>   Pasta, noodles
>   Pastry
>   Pizza bases
>   Pretzels
>   Semolina
>   Wheatgerm, Wheat bran, Wheat nuts.

Good replacements are easy to find

---

o   Alcohol – beer, ale, lager, gin and grain-based spirits
o   Beverages – cereal-based and malted beverages
o   Bread crumbed or battered meats and fish
o   Coated meats – with wheat flour before being browned
o   Fish canned in broth containing hydrolyzed vegetable protein (HVP) or hydrolyzed plant protein (HPP)
o   Sauces and gravy made with ingredients not allowed
    Sausages and hamburgers with gluten fillings
o   Soups – made with barley
o   Soy sauce made with wheat
o   Sweets – licorice, candies with ingredients not allowed.

Reading food labels

o   Do not assume that familiar foods will remain gluten-free as manufacturers often alter their recipes.

o   Avoid products of unknown origin such as "starch" or "modified starch". When in doubt, leave it out!

o   Manufacturers' ingredient lists may be out of date. Do not necessarily rely on them.

Ingredients must be listed on the label from the greatest to the smallest by weight. When there are very small amounts of multi-component ingredients (under 5%), then it is permitted to list the composite ingredient only. For example, chocolate might be listed rather than its individual components of cocoa, cocoa butter and sugar. But common food allergens must now be listed, however small their amount. Food additives must be identified, usually by number, and must be included in the ingredient list (see **www.foodstandards.govt.nz**).

Modifying your recipes

In many cases, you can modify your existing recipes for cakes and biscuits to make them gluten-free. Gluten is the substance in wheat that helps hold the basic ingredients together. This means that you will need to use other 'binding' agents. Gluten replacements include:

o   Replace the role of gluten with xanthan or guar gums.
o   Try adding some more baking powder to your cakes.
o   Adding an additional egg to GF pancake batters is good.
o   Try using "gluten-free gluten substitute".

Experiment, and accept that a few of your first attempts may be unsuccessful.

Gluten-free recipes for you – free

We would like to give you some recipes.
These are free for you. Just go to the website
www.doctorgluten.com
All you have to do is put in your user name
and password. Then you can get your free
recipes and much more information.

Go to **www.doctorgluten.com**

Your User name: **gluten**
Your Password: **free**

Then you can get your free recipes

❑The Energy Effect: Your Questions Answered

Dr Rodney Ford, nutritional and energy expert, teaches you how to live each day with High Energy. He shows you how to use the combination of your body, brain and spirit to create – The Energy Effect. Do you find that you lack time or energy to do all that you want? Do you want feel energized so you can keep going – and going – to the end of your day? The Energy Effect gives you complete answers on how to energize your life.

ISBN 0-476-00670-8 (192 pages)   (NZ$34.95 Aus$29.95 US$19.95)

❑Going Gluten-Free: How to Get Started

"Overwhelm" is often the first emotion felt when you are confronted by the prospect of a gluten-free diet. Find out how you can get started. Step1– Get ready: Identify if you really are gluten-sensitive. Check out your symptoms and blood tests. Step 2 – Get set up: Find out all about gluten. Use our shopping list to help you work out what you can eat and what you should avoid. Step 3 – Go gluten-free: Follow the recipes and eating ideas. Gluten-free can be a great experience.

ISBN 0-476-01020-9 (64 pages)   (NZ$14.95 Aus$14.95 US$9.95)

See our other books

❏Are You Gluten-Sensitive? Your Questions Answered

This book is based on the questions that I am so frequently asked by my patients. I answer their questions in detail and put them into the clinical context. There is lots of confusion about the diagnosis and management of people who are gluten-sensitive. This book has been written to clarify this muddle. It is full of practical information.

ISBN 0-476-00917-0 (192 pages)   (NZ$34.95 Aus$34.95 US$19.95)

❏The Gluten-Free Lunch Book

What can I have for lunch? That is our most often asked question. Easy and yummy lunches make all the difference if you are trying to stay gluten-free. We have brought together the best lunch ideas so that you never have to worry about lunch again. Simple and delicious gluten-free lunch box ideas for you and your family. Follow these recipes and eating ideas for a great gluten-free experience.

ISBN 0-473-10498-9 (64 pages)   (NZ$14.95 Aus$14.95 US$9.95)

❏The book for the Sick, Tired & Grumpy (Gluten-free kids)

Over 50 people tell their amazing stories. A cure for so many people who feel sick, tired or grumpy. These personal accounts are very moving with a raw honesty that hits home. If you want to feel well and full of energy again – then this book is for you. These children and parents tell about their low energy, their irritability and troublesome symptoms before they discovered their gluten-sensitivity. You then hear how going gluten-free has changed their lives. This might be just the answer you are looking for.

ISBN 0-473-10079-7 (192 pages)   (NZ$34.95 Aus$34.95 US$19.95)

❏Full Of It! The shocking truth about gluten

An alarming fact is that gluten can damage your brain. Have you ever wondered why you crave for another hunk of bread? If something that you ate was slowly eroding the function and the ability of your brain, then would you want to know what that food was? It could be gluten! Gluten is linked to ataxia, migraine, ADHD, autism, depression, epilepsy, mood and psychiatric disorders.   Gluten also can disrupt your brain's regulation of your gut – causing mayhem in your bowel. Gluten-sensitivity is a brain disease! Read the evidence for yourself.

ISBN 0-473-10407-5   (192 pages)   (NZ$34.95 Aus$34.95 US$19.95)

Available from our website: www.doctorgluten.com

BOOK ORDER FORM

☐Are You Gluten-Sensitive? Your Questions Answered

☐Going Gluten-Free: How to Get Started

☐The Gluten-Free Lunch Book

☐The book for the **Sick, Tired & Grumpy** (Gluten-free kids)

☐**Full of it! The shocking truth about gluten**

☐The Energy Effect? Your Questions Answered

(Please indicate the number of each book that you want to order. Prices stated on previous page)

Please add postage & handling: 1 book $7.00, 2 books $12, 3 or 4 books $15

(Prices for postage and handling to be paid in the currency of purchase)

Order for:

Name: _____

Postal address: _____

_____

Phone: _____   Fax: _____

Email: _____@_____

Number of books required: _____   Currency _____

Cost of books $ _____   Postage $ _____   Total $_____

Method of payment:

Cheque ☐   Visa ☐   MasterCard ☐   (please tick)

Cardholder's name: _____

Credit card number :_____

Signature: _____   Expiry date: _____/_____

Please make your cheque payable to:

Doctor Gluten, PO Box 25-360, Christchurch, New Zealand.

Fax orders: +64 3 3770596

Email orders: orders@doctorgluten.com

Web orders: www.doctorgluten.com

(Please allow 21 days for postal delivery)